50 French Restaurant Meals for Home

By: Kelly Johnson

Table of Contents

- Pumpernickel
- Pretzel (Brezn)
- Rye Bread (Roggenbrot)
- Bauernbrot (Farmer's Bread)
- Vollkornbrot (Whole Grain Bread)
- Brötchen (German Rolls)
- Schwarzbrot (Dark Bread)
- Zwiebelbrot (Onion Bread)
- Laugenspirale (Pretzel Spiral)
- Sourdough Bread (Sauerteigbrot)
- Kartoffelbrot (Potato Bread)
- Mohnbrötchen (Poppy Seed Rolls)
- Dinkelbrot (Spelt Bread)
- Kürbiskernbrot (Pumpkin Seed Bread)
- Bauernlaib (Farm Loaf)
- Sonnenblumenbrot (Sunflower Seed Bread)
- Laugenbrötchen (Pretzel Rolls)
- Kastenbrot (Loaf Bread)
- Apfelbrot (Apple Bread)
- Roggenmischbrot (Rye Mixed Bread)
- Butterzopf (Butter Braid)
- Birnenbrot (Pear Bread)
- Nussbrot (Nut Bread)
- Roggenmischlaib (Rye Mixed Loaf)
- Walnussbrot (Walnut Bread)
- Mühlenbrot (Mill Bread)
- Paderborner Brot
- Schwarzsauer (Dark Sourdough)
- Heidelbeerbrot (Blueberry Bread)
- Fruchtbrot (Fruit Bread)
- Knoblauchbrot (Garlic Bread)
- Bärlauchbrot (Wild Garlic Bread)
- Sesam Brot (Sesame Bread)
- Zuckerkuchen (Sugar Cake Bread)
- Birnen-Nussbrot (Pear Nut Bread)

- Mürbeteig Brot (Shortcrust Bread)
- Krustenbrot (Crusty Bread)
- Pflaumenbrot (Plum Bread)
- Hefegebäck (Yeast Pastries)
- Quarkbrot (Cottage Cheese Bread)
- Quarkzopf (Cottage Cheese Braid)
- Roggenbrot mit Schrot (Rye Bread with Bran)
- Brezelkuchen (Pretzel Cake)
- Kartoffelkruste (Potato Crust Bread)
- Alpensauerbrot (Alpine Sourdough)
- Frischkäsebrot (Cream Cheese Bread)
- Hirsebrot (Millet Bread)
- Dörrobstbrot (Dried Fruit Bread)
- Zuckerrübensirupbrot (Beet Syrup Bread)
- Marzipanbrot (Marzipan Bread)

Pumpernickel

Ingredients:

- 2 1/2 cups whole rye flour
- 1 cup all-purpose flour
- 1 tsp salt
- 2 tsp active dry yeast
- 1 1/2 cups warm water
- 2 tbsp molasses
- 1 tbsp brown sugar

Instructions:

1. In a large bowl, combine the rye flour, all-purpose flour, salt, and yeast.
2. In a separate bowl, mix the warm water, molasses, and brown sugar. Add this to the dry ingredients.
3. Mix until a sticky dough forms, then knead for about 8-10 minutes.
4. Cover and let the dough rise for 1-2 hours.
5. Preheat the oven to 375°F (190°C). Shape the dough into a round loaf and let it rise for 30 minutes.
6. Bake for 35-40 minutes until the bread is firm and the top is golden brown. Cool before slicing.

Pretzel (Brezn)

Ingredients:

- 3 1/2 cups all-purpose flour
- 1 tsp salt
- 1 packet active dry yeast
- 1 cup warm water
- 1 tbsp sugar
- 2 tbsp baking soda
- Coarse sea salt

Instructions:

1. In a bowl, combine flour, salt, yeast, warm water, and sugar. Mix until a dough forms.
2. Knead the dough for 10 minutes, then let it rise for 1 hour.
3. Preheat the oven to 450°F (230°C). Bring a large pot of water to a boil and add baking soda.
4. Divide the dough into equal portions and roll each into a rope. Twist into pretzel shapes and carefully dip each pretzel into the boiling water for about 30 seconds.
5. Place on a baking sheet, sprinkle with coarse sea salt, and bake for 15-20 minutes until golden brown.

Rye Bread (Roggenbrot)

Ingredients:

- 2 1/2 cups rye flour
- 1 1/2 cups all-purpose flour
- 1 tsp salt
- 2 tsp active dry yeast
- 1 1/2 cups warm water
- 1 tbsp honey

Instructions:

1. In a bowl, combine rye flour, all-purpose flour, salt, and yeast.
2. In a separate bowl, mix warm water and honey. Add to the dry ingredients.
3. Mix until a dough forms and knead for 8-10 minutes.
4. Let the dough rise for 1-2 hours.
5. Preheat the oven to 375°F (190°C). Shape the dough into a loaf and let it rise for 30 minutes.
6. Bake for 35-40 minutes, until the bread is firm and slightly crusty. Let cool before slicing.

Bauernbrot (Farmer's Bread)

Ingredients:

- 3 cups all-purpose flour
- 1 cup rye flour
- 1 1/2 tsp salt
- 1 packet active dry yeast
- 1 1/2 cups warm water
- 1 tbsp olive oil

Instructions:

1. Combine both flours, salt, and yeast in a bowl.
2. Add warm water and olive oil. Stir until a dough forms.
3. Knead for 8-10 minutes, then let rise for 1-2 hours.
4. Preheat the oven to 375°F (190°C). Shape the dough into a round loaf and let it rise for 30 minutes.
5. Bake for 30-35 minutes until the bread has a golden crust and sounds hollow when tapped.

Vollkornbrot (Whole Grain Bread)

Ingredients:

- 2 1/2 cups whole wheat flour
- 1 cup rye flour
- 1 tsp salt
- 1 packet active dry yeast
- 1 1/2 cups warm water
- 2 tbsp honey
- 2 tbsp sunflower seeds (optional)

Instructions:

1. In a bowl, mix the whole wheat flour, rye flour, salt, and yeast.
2. Add warm water and honey, mixing until a dough forms. Add sunflower seeds if desired.
3. Knead for 8-10 minutes. Let rise for 1-2 hours.
4. Preheat the oven to 375°F (190°C). Shape into a loaf and let rise for another 30 minutes.
5. Bake for 35-40 minutes until firm and golden. Cool before slicing.

Brötchen (German Rolls)

Ingredients:

- 3 cups all-purpose flour
- 1 tsp salt
- 1 packet active dry yeast
- 1 cup warm water
- 2 tbsp olive oil

Instructions:

1. In a large bowl, combine flour, salt, and yeast.
2. Add warm water and olive oil, stirring to form a dough.
3. Knead for 8 minutes and let rise for 1 hour.
4. Preheat the oven to 400°F (200°C). Shape the dough into small rolls and place on a baking sheet.
5. Let rise for 20-30 minutes, then bake for 15-20 minutes until golden brown.

Schwarzbrot (Dark Bread)

Ingredients:

- 2 1/2 cups whole rye flour
- 1 1/2 cups all-purpose flour
- 1 tsp salt
- 1 packet active dry yeast
- 1 1/2 cups warm water
- 2 tbsp molasses

Instructions:

1. Combine rye flour, all-purpose flour, salt, and yeast in a bowl.
2. Add warm water and molasses. Stir until a dough forms.
3. Knead for 8-10 minutes, then let rise for 1-2 hours.
4. Preheat the oven to 375°F (190°C). Shape into a loaf and let rise for 30 minutes.
5. Bake for 35-40 minutes, until the bread is firm and golden.

Zwiebelbrot (Onion Bread)

Ingredients:

- 3 cups all-purpose flour
- 1/2 cup finely chopped onions
- 1 tsp salt
- 1 packet active dry yeast
- 1 cup warm water
- 1 tbsp olive oil

Instructions:

1. In a bowl, combine flour, salt, yeast, and chopped onions.
2. Add warm water and olive oil, stirring to form a dough.
3. Knead for 8-10 minutes and let rise for 1-2 hours.
4. Preheat the oven to 375°F (190°C). Shape into a loaf and let rise for 30 minutes.
5. Bake for 30-35 minutes, until golden. Let cool before slicing.

Laugenspirale (Pretzel Spiral)

Ingredients:

- 3 1/2 cups all-purpose flour
- 1 tsp salt
- 1 packet active dry yeast
- 1 cup warm water
- 1 tbsp sugar
- 2 tbsp baking soda
- Coarse sea salt

Instructions:

1. In a bowl, combine flour, salt, yeast, warm water, and sugar.
2. Knead the dough for 10 minutes, then let rise for 1 hour.
3. Preheat the oven to 450°F (230°C). Bring a large pot of water to a boil and add baking soda.
4. Divide the dough into portions and roll into ropes. Twist each rope into a spiral shape.
5. Dip each spiral into the boiling water for about 30 seconds, then place on a baking sheet.
6. Sprinkle with coarse sea salt and bake for 15-20 minutes, until golden.

Sourdough Bread (Sauerteigbrot)

Ingredients:

- 2 cups sourdough starter
- 3 cups all-purpose flour
- 1 cup whole wheat flour
- 1 1/2 tsp salt
- 1 1/4 cups warm water

Instructions:

1. In a large bowl, combine the sourdough starter, all-purpose flour, whole wheat flour, salt, and warm water.
2. Mix until a dough forms and knead for 10 minutes until smooth.
3. Let the dough rise for 4-6 hours or overnight.
4. Preheat the oven to 450°F (230°C). Shape the dough into a round loaf and place it on a parchment-lined baking sheet.
5. Bake for 30-35 minutes until the bread is golden and sounds hollow when tapped.

Kartoffelbrot (Potato Bread)

Ingredients:

- 2 cups mashed potatoes (cooled)
- 4 cups all-purpose flour
- 1 tsp salt
- 1 packet active dry yeast
- 1 1/2 cups warm water
- 1 tbsp olive oil

Instructions:

1. In a large bowl, combine mashed potatoes, flour, salt, and yeast.
2. Add warm water and olive oil. Mix until a dough forms.
3. Knead for 8-10 minutes, then let rise for 1-2 hours.
4. Preheat the oven to 375°F (190°C). Shape the dough into a loaf and let rise for 30 minutes.
5. Bake for 35-40 minutes until golden and firm.

Mohnbrötchen (Poppy Seed Rolls)

Ingredients:

- 3 cups all-purpose flour
- 1 tsp salt
- 1 packet active dry yeast
- 1/4 cup sugar
- 1 cup warm milk
- 1/4 cup butter
- 1/4 cup poppy seeds

Instructions:

1. In a bowl, combine flour, salt, yeast, and sugar.
2. In a separate bowl, melt butter and mix with warm milk. Add this to the dry ingredients and stir until a dough forms.
3. Knead for 8 minutes, then let rise for 1 hour.
4. Preheat the oven to 375°F (190°C). Shape the dough into small rolls and place on a baking sheet.
5. Brush with milk and sprinkle with poppy seeds. Bake for 15-20 minutes until golden brown.

Dinkelbrot (Spelt Bread)

Ingredients:

- 3 cups spelt flour
- 1 1/2 tsp salt
- 1 packet active dry yeast
- 1 1/2 cups warm water
- 1 tbsp honey

Instructions:

1. In a large bowl, combine spelt flour, salt, and yeast.
2. Add warm water and honey, mixing until a dough forms.
3. Knead for 8-10 minutes, then let rise for 1-2 hours.
4. Preheat the oven to 375°F (190°C). Shape the dough into a loaf and let rise for 30 minutes.
5. Bake for 35-40 minutes, until golden and firm.

Kürbiskernbrot (Pumpkin Seed Bread)

Ingredients:

- 2 cups whole wheat flour
- 1 cup all-purpose flour
- 1/2 cup pumpkin seeds
- 1 tsp salt
- 1 packet active dry yeast
- 1 1/4 cups warm water
- 1 tbsp olive oil

Instructions:

1. In a bowl, combine the whole wheat flour, all-purpose flour, pumpkin seeds, salt, and yeast.
2. Add warm water and olive oil, mixing until a dough forms.
3. Knead for 8-10 minutes, then let rise for 1-2 hours.
4. Preheat the oven to 375°F (190°C). Shape the dough into a loaf and let rise for 30 minutes.
5. Bake for 35-40 minutes until golden and the top is slightly firm.

Bauernlaib (Farm Loaf)

Ingredients:

- 3 cups all-purpose flour
- 1 cup whole wheat flour
- 1 tsp salt
- 1 packet active dry yeast
- 1 1/2 cups warm water
- 1 tbsp honey

Instructions:

1. In a bowl, combine all-purpose flour, whole wheat flour, salt, and yeast.
2. Add warm water and honey, mixing until a dough forms.
3. Knead for 8-10 minutes and let rise for 1-2 hours.
4. Preheat the oven to 375°F (190°C). Shape the dough into a round loaf and let it rise for 30 minutes.
5. Bake for 35-40 minutes until golden brown.

Sonnenblumenbrot (Sunflower Seed Bread)

Ingredients:

- 3 cups all-purpose flour
- 1/2 cup sunflower seeds
- 1 tsp salt
- 1 packet active dry yeast
- 1 1/4 cups warm water
- 1 tbsp olive oil

Instructions:

1. In a large bowl, combine flour, sunflower seeds, salt, and yeast.
2. Add warm water and olive oil, mixing until a dough forms.
3. Knead for 8-10 minutes, then let rise for 1-2 hours.
4. Preheat the oven to 375°F (190°C). Shape the dough into a loaf and let rise for 30 minutes.
5. Bake for 35-40 minutes until golden and firm.

Laugenbrötchen (Pretzel Rolls)

Ingredients:

- 3 1/2 cups all-purpose flour
- 1 tsp salt
- 1 packet active dry yeast
- 1 cup warm water
- 2 tbsp sugar
- 2 tbsp baking soda
- Coarse sea salt

Instructions:

1. In a bowl, combine flour, salt, yeast, and sugar.
2. Add warm water and mix until a dough forms.
3. Knead for 8-10 minutes, then let rise for 1 hour.
4. Preheat the oven to 450°F (230°C). Bring a pot of water to a boil and add baking soda.
5. Shape the dough into rolls, then dip each into the boiling water for 30 seconds. Sprinkle with coarse sea salt.
6. Bake for 15-20 minutes until golden brown.

Kastenbrot (Loaf Bread)

Ingredients:

- 3 cups all-purpose flour
- 1 tsp salt
- 1 packet active dry yeast
- 1 1/2 cups warm water
- 1 tbsp honey

Instructions:

1. In a bowl, combine flour, salt, and yeast.
2. Add warm water and honey, mixing until a dough forms.
3. Knead for 8-10 minutes and let rise for 1-2 hours.
4. Preheat the oven to 375°F (190°C). Shape the dough into a loaf and place it in a greased loaf pan.
5. Let rise for 30 minutes, then bake for 35-40 minutes until golden brown.

Apfelbrot (Apple Bread)

Ingredients:

- 2 cups all-purpose flour
- 1/2 cup brown sugar
- 1 tsp cinnamon
- 1/2 tsp nutmeg
- 2 medium apples, peeled and chopped
- 1 packet active dry yeast
- 1/2 cup warm milk
- 1/4 cup butter

Instructions:

1. In a bowl, combine flour, brown sugar, cinnamon, and nutmeg.
2. Add the apples and yeast, then stir in warm milk and melted butter to form a dough.
3. Knead for 8 minutes, then let rise for 1 hour.
4. Preheat the oven to 375°F (190°C). Shape the dough into a loaf and let rise for 30 minutes.
5. Bake for 35-40 minutes until golden brown and firm.

Roggenmischbrot (Rye Mixed Bread)

Ingredients:

- 2 cups rye flour
- 2 cups all-purpose flour
- 1 1/2 tsp salt
- 1 packet active dry yeast
- 1 1/4 cups warm water
- 1 tbsp honey
- 1 tbsp caraway seeds (optional)

Instructions:

1. In a bowl, combine rye flour, all-purpose flour, salt, yeast, and caraway seeds (if using).
2. Add warm water and honey, and mix until a dough forms.
3. Knead for 8-10 minutes, then let the dough rise for 1-2 hours, or until doubled in size.
4. Preheat the oven to 375°F (190°C). Shape the dough into a round loaf or place it in a loaf pan.
5. Let it rise for an additional 30 minutes, then bake for 35-40 minutes until golden brown and firm to the touch.

Butterzopf (Butter Braid)

Ingredients:

- 3 1/2 cups all-purpose flour
- 1 packet active dry yeast
- 1/2 cup milk, warmed
- 1/2 cup butter, softened
- 1/4 cup sugar
- 2 eggs
- 1 tsp salt
- 1 egg (for egg wash)

Instructions:

1. In a bowl, combine flour, yeast, sugar, and salt.
2. Add the warm milk, butter, eggs, and mix until a dough forms.
3. Knead for 10 minutes, then let it rise for 1-2 hours until doubled in size.
4. Preheat the oven to 350°F (175°C).
5. Once risen, divide the dough into three parts and braid it. Place the braid on a parchment-lined baking sheet.
6. Brush the dough with a beaten egg for a golden finish and bake for 25-30 minutes, until golden brown.

Birnenbrot (Pear Bread)

Ingredients:

- 2 cups all-purpose flour
- 1/2 cup brown sugar
- 1 tsp ground cinnamon
- 1/2 tsp ground nutmeg
- 1 packet active dry yeast
- 1/2 cup warm milk
- 1/2 cup pear puree
- 1/2 cup butter, melted

Instructions:

1. In a bowl, mix flour, brown sugar, cinnamon, nutmeg, and yeast.
2. Add warm milk, pear puree, and melted butter, and stir to combine.
3. Knead for 8-10 minutes, then let rise for 1-2 hours.
4. Preheat the oven to 350°F (175°C). Shape the dough into a loaf and let it rise for 30 minutes.
5. Bake for 35-40 minutes until golden brown and firm to the touch.

Nussbrot (Nut Bread)

Ingredients:

- 2 cups all-purpose flour
- 1/2 cup mixed nuts (walnuts, hazelnuts, almonds)
- 1 tsp salt
- 1 packet active dry yeast
- 1/2 cup warm water
- 1 tbsp honey

Instructions:

1. In a bowl, combine flour, salt, yeast, and mixed nuts.
2. Add warm water and honey, and mix until a dough forms.
3. Knead for 8 minutes, then let rise for 1-2 hours.
4. Preheat the oven to 375°F (190°C). Shape the dough into a loaf and let it rise for 30 minutes.
5. Bake for 35-40 minutes until golden brown and firm.

Roggenmischlaib (Rye Mixed Loaf)

Ingredients:

- 1 1/2 cups rye flour
- 1 1/2 cups all-purpose flour
- 1 tsp salt
- 1 packet active dry yeast
- 1 1/4 cups warm water
- 1 tbsp honey

Instructions:

1. In a bowl, combine rye flour, all-purpose flour, salt, and yeast.
2. Add warm water and honey, and mix until a dough forms.
3. Knead for 8-10 minutes, then let rise for 1-2 hours.
4. Preheat the oven to 375°F (190°C). Shape the dough into a loaf and let it rise for 30 minutes.
5. Bake for 35-40 minutes until golden and firm.

Walnussbrot (Walnut Bread)

Ingredients:

- 3 cups all-purpose flour
- 1/2 cup chopped walnuts
- 1 tsp salt
- 1 packet active dry yeast
- 1 1/4 cups warm water
- 1 tbsp olive oil

Instructions:

1. In a bowl, combine flour, walnuts, salt, and yeast.
2. Add warm water and olive oil, and stir to combine.
3. Knead for 8-10 minutes, then let rise for 1-2 hours.
4. Preheat the oven to 375°F (190°C). Shape the dough into a loaf and let it rise for 30 minutes.
5. Bake for 35-40 minutes until golden brown.

Mühlenbrot (Mill Bread)

Ingredients:

- 2 cups whole wheat flour
- 1 cup all-purpose flour
- 1 tsp salt
- 1 packet active dry yeast
- 1 1/4 cups warm water
- 1 tbsp olive oil

Instructions:

1. In a bowl, combine whole wheat flour, all-purpose flour, salt, and yeast.
2. Add warm water and olive oil, and mix until a dough forms.
3. Knead for 8-10 minutes, then let rise for 1-2 hours.
4. Preheat the oven to 375°F (190°C). Shape the dough into a loaf and let it rise for 30 minutes.
5. Bake for 35-40 minutes until golden brown.

Paderborner Brot

Ingredients:

- 2 1/2 cups all-purpose flour
- 1 1/2 cups whole wheat flour
- 1 tsp salt
- 1 packet active dry yeast
- 1 1/4 cups warm water
- 1 tbsp honey

Instructions:

1. In a bowl, combine both flours, salt, and yeast.
2. Add warm water and honey, and stir until a dough forms.
3. Knead for 8-10 minutes, then let rise for 1-2 hours.
4. Preheat the oven to 375°F (190°C). Shape the dough into a round loaf and let it rise for 30 minutes.
5. Bake for 35-40 minutes until golden and firm.

Schwarzsauer (Dark Sourdough)

Ingredients:

- 2 cups rye flour
- 1 1/2 cups all-purpose flour
- 1 packet active dry yeast
- 1 1/4 cups warm water
- 1 tbsp sugar
- 2 tbsp molasses or dark honey

Instructions:

1. In a bowl, combine rye flour, all-purpose flour, yeast, and sugar.
2. Add warm water and molasses, and stir until a dough forms.
3. Knead for 8-10 minutes, then let rise for 1-2 hours.
4. Preheat the oven to 375°F (190°C). Shape the dough into a loaf and let it rise for 30 minutes.
5. Bake for 35-40 minutes until golden and firm.

Heidelbeerbrot (Blueberry Bread)

Ingredients:

- 2 cups all-purpose flour
- 1/2 cup sugar
- 1 tsp baking powder
- 1/2 tsp baking soda
- 1/4 tsp salt
- 1/2 cup unsalted butter, softened
- 1/2 cup milk
- 1 egg
- 1 1/2 cups fresh or frozen blueberries

Instructions:

1. Preheat the oven to 350°F (175°C). Grease and flour a loaf pan.
2. In a bowl, combine flour, sugar, baking powder, baking soda, and salt.
3. In another bowl, whisk together butter, milk, and egg. Add the wet ingredients to the dry ingredients and stir to combine.
4. Gently fold in the blueberries.
5. Pour the batter into the prepared loaf pan and bake for 45-50 minutes, or until a toothpick inserted comes out clean.
6. Let it cool in the pan for 10 minutes before transferring it to a wire rack to cool completely.

Fruchtbrot (Fruit Bread)

Ingredients:

- 2 cups all-purpose flour
- 1/2 cup dried fruit (raisins, apricots, or mixed fruit)
- 1/4 cup sugar
- 1/2 tsp cinnamon
- 1/2 tsp salt
- 1 packet active dry yeast
- 1 1/4 cups warm water
- 2 tbsp butter, melted

Instructions:

1. In a large bowl, mix flour, dried fruit, sugar, cinnamon, and salt.
2. In a separate bowl, dissolve the yeast in warm water and let it sit for 5 minutes.
3. Add the yeast mixture and melted butter to the flour mixture. Stir to form a dough.
4. Knead for 8-10 minutes, then let it rise for 1-2 hours until doubled in size.
5. Preheat the oven to 375°F (190°C).
6. Shape the dough into a loaf and place it on a greased baking sheet. Let it rise for 30 minutes.
7. Bake for 30-35 minutes until golden brown and firm to the touch.

Knoblauchbrot (Garlic Bread)

Ingredients:

- 1 loaf of French or Italian bread
- 1/2 cup unsalted butter, softened
- 4 cloves garlic, minced
- 2 tbsp chopped fresh parsley
- Salt, to taste

Instructions:

1. Preheat the oven to 375°F (190°C).
2. Slice the loaf of bread in half lengthwise.
3. In a small bowl, mix butter, garlic, parsley, and salt.
4. Spread the garlic butter evenly on both halves of the bread.
5. Place the bread on a baking sheet and bake for 10-12 minutes until the edges are crispy and golden brown.

Bärlauchbrot (Wild Garlic Bread)

Ingredients:

- 2 cups all-purpose flour
- 1 packet active dry yeast
- 1 tsp salt
- 1/2 cup warm water
- 2 tbsp olive oil
- 1/4 cup fresh wild garlic leaves, finely chopped

Instructions:

1. In a large bowl, combine flour, yeast, and salt.
2. Add warm water and olive oil, stirring to form a dough.
3. Knead for 8-10 minutes, then let rise for 1-2 hours until doubled.
4. Preheat the oven to 375°F (190°C).
5. Gently fold in the chopped wild garlic leaves. Shape the dough into a loaf and place it on a greased baking sheet.
6. Let it rise for 30 minutes before baking for 30-35 minutes, until golden brown.

Sesam Brot (Sesame Bread)

Ingredients:

- 2 cups all-purpose flour
- 1/2 cup sesame seeds
- 1 tsp salt
- 1 packet active dry yeast
- 1 1/4 cups warm water
- 1 tbsp olive oil

Instructions:

1. In a large bowl, combine flour, sesame seeds, salt, and yeast.
2. Add warm water and olive oil, mixing to form a dough.
3. Knead for 8-10 minutes, then let rise for 1-2 hours.
4. Preheat the oven to 375°F (190°C).
5. Shape the dough into a loaf and let it rise for 30 minutes.
6. Bake for 35-40 minutes until golden brown.

Zuckerkuchen (Sugar Cake Bread)

Ingredients:

- 2 cups all-purpose flour
- 1/2 cup sugar
- 1 tsp baking powder
- 1/2 tsp salt
- 1/4 cup butter, softened
- 1 egg
- 1/2 cup milk
- 1 tsp vanilla extract

Instructions:

1. Preheat the oven to 350°F (175°C). Grease and flour a loaf pan.
2. In a bowl, combine flour, sugar, baking powder, and salt.
3. In another bowl, beat butter, egg, milk, and vanilla extract.
4. Add the wet ingredients to the dry ingredients and stir until smooth.
5. Pour the batter into the prepared pan and bake for 30-35 minutes until golden brown.

Birnen-Nussbrot (Pear Nut Bread)

Ingredients:

- 2 cups all-purpose flour
- 1/2 cup chopped pears
- 1/2 cup chopped walnuts
- 1/2 cup sugar
- 1 tsp baking powder
- 1/2 tsp cinnamon
- 1/2 tsp salt
- 1 packet active dry yeast
- 1/2 cup warm water
- 1 tbsp honey

Instructions:

1. Preheat the oven to 375°F (190°C). Grease a loaf pan.
2. In a bowl, combine flour, pears, walnuts, sugar, baking powder, cinnamon, salt, and yeast.
3. Add warm water and honey, stirring until a dough forms.
4. Knead the dough for 8-10 minutes, then let it rise for 1-2 hours.
5. Shape the dough into a loaf, place it in the pan, and let it rise for 30 minutes.
6. Bake for 35-40 minutes until golden and firm.

Mürbeteig Brot (Shortcrust Bread)

Ingredients:

- 2 cups all-purpose flour
- 1/2 cup butter, cold and cubed
- 1/4 cup sugar
- 1 egg yolk
- 1/4 cup cold water

Instructions:

1. Preheat the oven to 350°F (175°C). Grease a loaf pan.
2. In a food processor, pulse flour, butter, sugar, and egg yolk until it resembles breadcrumbs.
3. Add cold water and pulse until the dough forms.
4. Roll the dough out and shape it into a loaf, then bake for 25-30 minutes until golden.

Krustenbrot (Crusty Bread)

Ingredients:

- 3 cups all-purpose flour
- 1 packet active dry yeast
- 1 1/4 cups warm water
- 1 tbsp salt
- 1 tbsp olive oil

Instructions:

1. In a bowl, combine flour, yeast, salt, and olive oil.
2. Gradually add warm water, mixing to form a dough.
3. Knead for 8-10 minutes, then let rise for 1-2 hours.
4. Preheat the oven to 450°F (230°C) and place a baking stone or sheet inside.
5. Shape the dough into a round loaf and score the top with a knife.
6. Bake for 30-35 minutes until golden brown and crisp.

Pflaumenbrot (Plum Bread)

Ingredients:

- 2 cups all-purpose flour
- 1/2 cup sugar
- 1 tsp baking powder
- 1/2 tsp cinnamon
- 1/2 tsp salt
- 1/2 cup unsalted butter, softened
- 1/2 cup milk
- 2 eggs
- 1 1/2 cups fresh plums, chopped
- 1/4 cup chopped almonds (optional)

Instructions:

1. Preheat the oven to 350°F (175°C). Grease and flour a loaf pan.
2. In a bowl, combine flour, sugar, baking powder, cinnamon, and salt.
3. In another bowl, whisk together butter, milk, and eggs.
4. Add the wet ingredients to the dry ingredients and stir until combined.
5. Gently fold in the chopped plums and almonds.
6. Pour the batter into the prepared pan and bake for 45-50 minutes or until a toothpick comes out clean.
7. Let it cool in the pan for 10 minutes before transferring to a wire rack to cool completely.

Hefegebäck (Yeast Pastries)

Ingredients:

- 4 cups all-purpose flour
- 1 packet active dry yeast
- 1/2 cup sugar
- 1 tsp salt
- 1/2 cup milk
- 1/2 cup butter, melted
- 2 eggs
- 1 tsp vanilla extract

Instructions:

1. In a bowl, combine flour, yeast, sugar, and salt.
2. In a separate bowl, warm the milk and melted butter together. Add the eggs and vanilla extract.
3. Gradually mix the wet ingredients into the dry ingredients to form a dough.
4. Knead the dough for 8-10 minutes until smooth, then let it rise for 1-2 hours until doubled.
5. Preheat the oven to 375°F (190°C).
6. Roll the dough out and cut into your desired shapes (circular or square).
7. Place the pastries on a greased baking sheet, and bake for 12-15 minutes, until golden brown.

Quarkbrot (Cottage Cheese Bread)

Ingredients:

- 2 cups all-purpose flour
- 1 packet active dry yeast
- 1 tsp salt
- 1/2 cup quark (or substitute with cottage cheese)
- 1/2 cup warm water
- 2 tbsp olive oil

Instructions:

1. In a bowl, combine flour, yeast, and salt.
2. Add the quark, warm water, and olive oil. Mix to form a dough.
3. Knead for 8-10 minutes until the dough is smooth, then let it rise for 1-2 hours.
4. Preheat the oven to 375°F (190°C).
5. Shape the dough into a round loaf or desired shape, then place it on a greased baking sheet.
6. Let the dough rise for 30 minutes, then bake for 30-35 minutes, or until golden brown.

Quarkzopf (Cottage Cheese Braid)

Ingredients:

- 3 cups all-purpose flour
- 1 packet active dry yeast
- 1/4 cup sugar
- 1 tsp salt
- 1 cup quark (or cottage cheese)
- 1/4 cup milk
- 2 tbsp butter, softened
- 1 egg (for egg wash)

Instructions:

1. In a bowl, combine flour, yeast, sugar, and salt.
2. In another bowl, mix quark, milk, and butter.
3. Gradually add the wet ingredients to the dry ingredients to form a dough.
4. Knead the dough for 8-10 minutes until smooth, then let it rise for 1-2 hours.
5. Preheat the oven to 375°F (190°C).
6. Divide the dough into three equal pieces, roll them into ropes, and braid them.
7. Place the braided dough on a greased baking sheet, brush with an egg wash, and bake for 30-35 minutes until golden.

Roggenbrot mit Schrot (Rye Bread with Bran)

Ingredients:

- 2 cups rye flour
- 1 cup whole wheat flour
- 1/2 cup bran
- 1 packet active dry yeast
- 1 tsp salt
- 1 tbsp caraway seeds (optional)
- 1 1/4 cups warm water
- 1 tbsp honey

Instructions:

1. In a bowl, combine rye flour, whole wheat flour, bran, yeast, salt, and caraway seeds (if using).
2. In a separate bowl, mix warm water and honey.
3. Gradually add the wet ingredients to the dry ingredients and knead for 8-10 minutes until smooth.
4. Let the dough rise for 1-2 hours until doubled in size.
5. Preheat the oven to 375°F (190°C).
6. Shape the dough into a loaf and place it on a greased baking sheet. Let it rise for 30 minutes.
7. Bake for 30-35 minutes until firm and golden.

Brezelkuchen (Pretzel Cake)

Ingredients:

- 2 cups all-purpose flour
- 1/2 cup butter, softened
- 1/4 cup sugar
- 1 packet active dry yeast
- 1 tsp baking powder
- 1/4 cup milk
- 1 egg, beaten (for egg wash)
- Coarse salt, for sprinkling

Instructions:

1. Preheat the oven to 350°F (175°C). Grease a round cake pan.
2. In a bowl, combine flour, butter, sugar, yeast, and baking powder.
3. Add milk and mix until the dough forms.
4. Knead the dough for 5 minutes, then roll it out to fit the cake pan.
5. Brush the top with the beaten egg and sprinkle with coarse salt.
6. Bake for 25-30 minutes until golden brown.

Kartoffelkruste (Potato Crust Bread)

Ingredients:

- 2 cups all-purpose flour
- 1/2 cup mashed potatoes (cooled)
- 1 packet active dry yeast
- 1 tsp salt
- 1 tbsp olive oil
- 1/2 cup warm water

Instructions:

1. In a bowl, combine flour, mashed potatoes, yeast, and salt.
2. Add warm water and olive oil, stirring to form a dough.
3. Knead for 8-10 minutes until smooth, then let rise for 1-2 hours.
4. Preheat the oven to 375°F (190°C).
5. Shape the dough into a loaf and place it on a greased baking sheet. Let it rise for 30 minutes.
6. Bake for 30-35 minutes until golden brown and firm.

Alpensauerbrot (Alpine Sourdough)

Ingredients:

- 2 cups rye flour
- 1 cup all-purpose flour
- 1 packet active dry yeast
- 1 tsp salt
- 1/2 tsp caraway seeds
- 1 1/4 cups warm water
- 1 tbsp sourdough starter (optional)

Instructions:

1. In a large bowl, mix rye flour, all-purpose flour, yeast, salt, and caraway seeds.
2. Add the warm water and sourdough starter (if using), and stir until the dough comes together.
3. Knead the dough for about 10 minutes until smooth.
4. Cover and let the dough rise for 1-2 hours, or until doubled in size.
5. Preheat the oven to 375°F (190°C).
6. Shape the dough into a round loaf and place it on a greased baking sheet.
7. Bake for 30-35 minutes or until golden and hollow when tapped on the bottom.

Frischkäsebrot (Cream Cheese Bread)

Ingredients:

- 2 cups all-purpose flour
- 1 packet active dry yeast
- 1 tsp salt
- 1/2 cup cream cheese, softened
- 1/4 cup milk
- 1/4 cup warm water
- 1 tbsp sugar

Instructions:

1. In a bowl, combine flour, yeast, and salt.
2. In another bowl, mix cream cheese, milk, warm water, and sugar.
3. Gradually add the wet mixture to the dry ingredients, stirring to form a dough.
4. Knead for about 8 minutes until smooth and elastic.
5. Let the dough rise for 1-2 hours, or until doubled.
6. Preheat the oven to 375°F (190°C).
7. Shape the dough into a loaf and place it in a greased loaf pan.
8. Let it rise for another 30 minutes, then bake for 25-30 minutes, or until golden and firm.

Hirsebrot (Millet Bread)

Ingredients:

- 1 cup millet flour
- 1 cup all-purpose flour
- 1 packet active dry yeast
- 1 tsp salt
- 1/4 cup honey
- 1 cup warm water

Instructions:

1. In a large bowl, combine millet flour, all-purpose flour, yeast, and salt.
2. Add honey and warm water to the mixture and stir until a dough forms.
3. Knead the dough for 10 minutes, then cover and let it rise for 1-2 hours.
4. Preheat the oven to 375°F (190°C).
5. Shape the dough into a loaf and place it on a greased baking sheet.
6. Let it rise for another 30 minutes, then bake for 30-35 minutes or until golden brown.

Dörrobstbrot (Dried Fruit Bread)

Ingredients:

- 2 cups all-purpose flour
- 1/2 cup raisins
- 1/2 cup dried apricots, chopped
- 1/4 cup walnuts, chopped
- 1 packet active dry yeast
- 1 tsp salt
- 1/2 cup warm water
- 1 tbsp honey

Instructions:

1. In a bowl, combine flour, raisins, apricots, walnuts, yeast, and salt.
2. In another bowl, mix warm water and honey.
3. Gradually add the wet mixture to the dry ingredients, stirring to form a dough.
4. Knead the dough for 10 minutes, then cover and let it rise for 1-2 hours.
5. Preheat the oven to 375°F (190°C).
6. Shape the dough into a round loaf and place it on a greased baking sheet.
7. Let it rise for another 30 minutes, then bake for 30-35 minutes or until golden brown.

Zuckerrübensirupbrot (Beet Syrup Bread)

Ingredients:

- 2 cups all-purpose flour
- 1 packet active dry yeast
- 1/2 cup beet syrup (or molasses)
- 1 tsp salt
- 1/4 cup warm water

Instructions:

1. In a bowl, combine flour, yeast, and salt.
2. In a separate bowl, mix beet syrup and warm water.
3. Gradually add the wet mixture to the dry ingredients and stir to form a dough.
4. Knead the dough for about 10 minutes until smooth.
5. Let it rise for 1-2 hours, or until doubled.
6. Preheat the oven to 375°F (190°C).
7. Shape the dough into a loaf and place it in a greased loaf pan.
8. Let it rise for 30 minutes, then bake for 25-30 minutes, or until golden and firm.

Marzipanbrot (Marzipan Bread)

Ingredients:

- 2 cups all-purpose flour
- 1 packet active dry yeast
- 1/4 cup sugar
- 1 tsp salt
- 1/2 cup marzipan, chopped into small pieces
- 1/2 cup warm water
- 1/4 cup milk
- 1 egg (for egg wash)

Instructions:

1. In a large bowl, combine flour, yeast, sugar, and salt.
2. In a separate bowl, mix warm water and milk.
3. Gradually add the wet mixture to the dry ingredients and stir to form a dough.
4. Knead for about 10 minutes until smooth, then fold in the chopped marzipan.
5. Let the dough rise for 1-2 hours, or until doubled.
6. Preheat the oven to 375°F (190°C).
7. Shape the dough into a loaf and place it on a greased baking sheet.
8. Brush the top with an egg wash, then bake for 25-30 minutes, or until golden brown.

www.ingramcontent.com/pod-product-compliance
Lightning Source LLC
LaVergne TN
LVHW081500060526
838201LV00056BA/2845